Fast Facts About Dogs

Fast Facts About BEAGLES

by Marcie Aboff

PEBBLE
a capstone imprint

Pebble Emerge is published by Pebble, an imprint of Capstone.
1710 Roe Crest Drive
North Mankato, Minnesota 56003
www.capstonepub.com

Library of Congress Cataloging-in-Publication Data is available on the Library of Congress website.
ISBN 978-1-9771-2454-8 (library binding)
ISBN 978-1-9771-2497-5 (eBook PDF)

Summary: Calling all beagle fans! Ever wondered about a beagle's personality? Want to find out the best way to care for this type of dog? Kids will learn all about beagles with fun facts, beautiful photos, and an activity.

Image Credits
Capstone Press/Karon Dubke, 20; Getty Images: Hulton Archive/Stringer, 18, PAUL J. RICHARDS/Staff, 13; iStockphoto: eAlisa, 10, Igorr1, 11; Shutterstock: Africa Studio, back cover, anetapics, 16, ARENA Creative, 15, bbernard, 5, Igor Normann, 9, Ivanova N, 6, Lunja 19, Plotitsyna NiNa, 7, Sandra Huber, cover, tetiana_u, 17, Wynian, cover (bottom)

Artistic elements: Shutterstock: Anbel, Ponysaurus

Editorial Credits
Editor: Megan Peterson; Designer: Sarah Bennett; Media Researcher: Kelly Garvin; Production Specialist: Tori Abraham

Printed in the United States of America.
3342

Table of Contents

Words in **bold** are in the glossary.

The Nose Knows!

Beagles follow their nose! These dogs have a great sense of smell. They will follow a **scent** anywhere. Beagles are clever too. They are cheerful. Families love these playful **hound** dogs.

4

Beagles have long, floppy ears. Their eyes are big. They have a smooth **double coat**. Their fur is white, black, and tan. Their fur might also have some yellow or red.

Beagles come in two sizes. Smaller ones stand up to 13 inches (33 centimeters) tall. They weigh less than 20 pounds (9 kilograms). Larger beagles stand up to 15 inches (38 cm) tall. They weigh up to 35 pounds (16 kg).

Beagle History

The first beagles came from England in the 1500s. They chased rabbits for hunters. Beagles came to the United States in the late 1800s. Hunters liked these scent hounds. Today beagles still help hunters. They are also a **popular** family pet.

Beagles at Home and Work

Beagles are a **pack** dog. They like to be with their human family. But they should always have a fence in the yard. Beagles could wander off without a fence. They might follow a scent down the street!

Beagles do not like being left alone too long. They will get bored. They might dig. They might howl. Their howling is called baying. It is a loud cry. They want their owner to come back!

Beagles help the U.S. government. Some work at airports as scent dogs. They help police in baggage areas. These beagles wear special vests. They sniff suitcases to find harmful foods. These foods might make people sick. Police throw these foods away.

Keeping Beagles Healthy

Beagles are usually healthy dogs. They need to visit the **veterinarian** once a year. Beagles can have hip problems. They can also have heart or back problems.

The vet checks their hips, hearts, and backs. The vet checks other things too. Beagles live about 10 to 15 years.

Caring for Beagles

Beagle puppies should be trained early. Sometimes they don't listen. Reward them with dog treats when they behave. But be careful. Beagles are also called chowhounds. They can overeat. Sometimes they sneak food from the garbage!

Beagles are an active **breed**. They need daily **exercise**. Beagles love going on long walks. Their fur should be brushed weekly. Keep their long ears clean. Bathe them as needed. Brush their teeth a few times a week.

Fun Facts About Beagles

- Most beagles have a white tip on their tail. The white tip helps hunters find them in tall grass.

- Former president Lyndon B. Johnson had three beagles. Their names were Him, Her, and Edgar.

- Beagles' long ears help trap smells. When they bend down, their ears touch their nose.

- Beagle means "loudmouth" in French.

- The comic strip dog Snoopy is a beagle.

Chase the Bottle Toy

What You Need:

- one empty plastic milk or water bottle
- dog treats that fit inside

What You Do:

1. Remove the bottle cap. Throw it away.

2. Put about 10 small dog treats inside the bottle.

3. Toss the bottle to your dog.

4. Watch your dog play with the bottle to get the treats. Yum!

Glossary

breed (BREED)—a certain kind of animal within an animal group

double coat (DUH-buhl KOHT)—a coat that is thick and soft close to the skin and covered with lighter, silky fur on the surface

exercise (EK-suhr-syz)—physical activity done in order to stay healthy and fit

hound (HOWND)—a type of dog that is often trained to hunt

pack (PAK)—a small group of animals that hunts together

popular (POP-yuh-lur)—liked or enjoyed by many people

scent (SENT)—the smell of something

veterinarian (vet-ur-uh-NAYR-ee-uhn)—a doctor trained to take care of animals

Read More

Frank, Sarah. *Beagles*. Minneapolis: Lerner Publications, 2020.

Rustad, Martha E.H. *Beagles*. Mankato, MN: Amicus High Interest/Amicus Ink, 2018.

Storm, Marysa. *Beagles*. Mankato, MN: Black Rabbit Books, 2021.

Internet Sites

American Kennel Club
https://www.akc.org/dog-breeds/beagle/

Animal Planet
http://www.animalplanet.com/breed-selector/dog-breeds/hound/beagle.html

Dogtime
https://dogtime.com/dog-breeds/beagle#/slide/1

Index